MYMUNA MAJIK AND THE BROKEN PUMP

KAZ

Copyright © 2024 by

KAZ

ALL RIGHTS RESERVED. NO part of this book may be reproduced or transmitted in any form by any means, electronic or mechanical, including photocopying and recording, or by any information storage and retrieval system, except as may be expressly permitted in writing from the author.

ISBN:
Paperback: 978-1-964898-48-3
eBook: 978-1-964898-42-1

Published by:
Pine Book Writing
www.PineBookWriting.com
R-10225 Yonge St Suite #250, Richmond Hill, ON L4C 3B2, Canada.

Printed in the United States of America

Disclaimer

This is a work of fiction. Names, characters, places and incidents are either a product of the author's imagination or are used fictitiously.

Acknowledgments

I thank the following who gave me what I needed to write and finish this book:

Yanten Masasi Thoronka from Bo Town, Sierra Leone: the inspiration behind the main protagonist of this book and cover photo model.

Izön Zale Thoronka, who provided new ideas and insights whenever things got stuck in the mud. And who shares many characteristics with Mukpasi (his Limba name).

Rhonda Lee, who inspired me with her own love for children's books, and provided editing and publishing ideas, rooting for me all the way to the finish line.

The Late Ma Musu Allieu, who provided spiritual guidance, miraculously and unbeknownst at first.

Martha McCamy, who helped me realize the need to bring this story back to life.

Marion Bundu, who prayed for this book.

Anika Kalk Derby, who helped spice up the storyline in Chapter 4.

Haja Mamie Bockarie, an inspirational community activist and head of Concerned Mothers' Movement for Women's Participation in Development in Bo, Sierra Leone.

Tererai Trent, the internationally recognized activist and author from Zimbabwe. Her book, 'The Girl Who Buried Her Dreams in a Can,' is referenced in this story.

My furry sidekicks who provide daily doses joy: **Fievel Boseman** and **Sweet Peet**.

Finally,

All of us who stick together, even when the well runs dry.

Table of Contents

Chapter 1: The Broken Pump 1

Chapter 2: Down By The River 12

Chapter 3: Poo Poo Germs 15

Chapter 4: Coconut Water 17

Chapter 5: Muddy Waters 28

Chapter 6: Fix the Pump 30

Chapter 7: Prevention 35

Chapter 1: The Broken Pump

Mymuna Majik would have loved to sleep an extra hour, or even an extra five minutes. But the call of the mosque, the cockle of the rooster, the bah of the goats, and the moo of the cows would not wait for her dream to end. The sun had not yet risen, and the air was crisp and damp. There was a cool Harmattan wind that brushed over her dry, cracked skin. Mymuna (nicknamed "My") pulled her mosquito net from under her foam mattress and tied it into a knot above her bed. She haphazardly stepped into her green plastic slippers as she petted the top of her dog Restore's head. She walked outside into the cool air, and took a deep breath. The wood burning from the outdoor kitchen made her stomach growl. Mymuna loved breakfast time, especially when her mother, Mama Majik, made her favorite: chapatis from East Africa. My's family lived in the small West African country of Sierra Leone, but Mama Majik often got to travel to other African countries through her job with the United Nations (known as the "UN"). She had learned about Swahili cooking on one of her trips to Tanzania, on the eastern coast of the African continent. Chapatis were a warm, crispy, somewhat sweet flat bread made from flour and water. After the first taste, they became a Majik family breakfast favorite. As My rubbed the sand out of her eyes that accumulated during her sleep, she heard that famous chime from around the back of the compound: "dah dah dah... BBC World News Radio!" The sound was familiar, something she associated with early mornings in her home.

Out back, Mister Majik, her father, sat on a tree trunk with a small, broken mirror in one hand, and a razor blade in the other. Mymuna entered the compound slowly, cautious not to scare her father. She didn't want him to make a mistake and cut himself while shaving.

"Good Morning Pa," said Mymuna as she rinsed Restore's water dish, filling it with fresh water from the bucket.

"Good Morning My," Mister Majik replied. "How did you sleep?"

"Fine. Only I had a funny dream."

"What was it?"

"I dreamt we were swimming in the river."

"Oh?" responded Mister, curiously.

"Yes, but the river was actually mud."

"Mud? That doesn't sound very pleasant."

"No." My thought for a minute. "Pa?" she continued, anxious to ask him a deep question.

"What is it my dear?"

"Do you believe that dreams are signs?"

"Ha Ha Ha!" Mister Majik had a very distinct and hearty laugh.

"Signs from whom?" he replied.

My tried to be serious and ignore his tone that suggested what she was asking was nonsense. "I don't know, from God, Allah, Yaweh, Buddha, Krishna, Mami Wata, someone like that."

"So young lady, what do you think your muddy river was all about?"

"I'm not sure yet." My began to feel sheepish, but she knew deep in her heart that this was another one of her intuitions. It is not the first time this happened. She had several dreams that turned out to be a preconception of things to come. And she was the only one in town besides Ma Musu (her granny) who could talk to the River Guardian, Barack the Crock. Everyone knew that Ma Musu had special powers that allowed her to heal and protect people through her connection with the River Guardian. My was certain she carried this gene, as she also could communicate with Barack the Crock. But she did not like to talk too much about that, for fear of being teased or envied.

Mister Majik pushed her along… "Well, you let me know when you figure it out. Until then, go wake your brother and fetch the water for your bath. You have school today. Don't want to be late!"

Mymuna followed orders and went to wake her six-year-old brother Mukpasi, nicknamed Muki. They lived in the peri-urban town of Bok in the coastal country of Sierra Leone, divided between lush rainforests, lowland plains, mountains in the north, and the Atlantic ocean in the South. Bok was surrounded by medicinal forests, used by the traditional healers to cure everything from malaria to witchcraft. And it had plenty of coconut trees.

My had a very spirited personality. She sometimes got criticized by her teachers for wanting to "run the show," taking charge of everything including acting like a busy-body and telling other kids what to do. This was particularly a problem for her in class 1 and 2. Since reaching class 3, however, she started to mature and knew her place as a student. She began respecting the teacher's role and asked how she could best help, rather than jumping in and taking charge. My was one of the brightest in her class, and in fact, all of Bok. She had a hard time focusing as she really enjoyed games and toys, but her uncle, Koro Thoro, had been working with her to improve her concentration. He would give her daily mathematics assignments and not allow her to climb guava trees until she had finished each daily lesson. At first, My despised the assignments. But after discovering how smart she was, she began to enjoy them. Although, she still preferred to climb trees and play with toy cars if she had a choice.

December had just started, and Mymuna was half-way done with class 3. She always knew when this time came because the weather began to change. During the months of December to May, the sweltering sun gave people in most parts of the country a break from the heat at dusk and dawn. My had to apply oil to her skin much more frequently, as it became dry from the lack of moisture in the air. Her skin was normally smooth, shiny and brown with a tint of gold. She had a small scar below her lip from the time she fell from a guava tree as a child. She had a long, lean figure, commonly referred to as "straight cut." She sometimes got teased for this shape, as most people liked to have a bit more 'body,' which was a sign of good health. But she knew it was genetic, something she got from her granny, and did not let it bother her. This is because her doctor told her that there was absolutely nothing wrong with her shape, and that she was pleased to see that My was involved in sports, and that she ate vegetables, some sort of protein such as groundnuts or beans, and a variety of fruit every day. And ate rice daily with traditional soup of course. Oh, and maybe some puff-puff (doughnut) here and there.

During the month of December, the cool, dry winds that blew off the Sahara Desert could be so brisk that people had to wear thick, warm, polyester jackets stuffed with cotton. My and Muki heard that these jackets came from a part of the United States called the 'Mid-West,' where their cousin Issata lived. Issata lived with her mother and step-father in a place called Madison, Wisconsin, which is one of the coldest places in the world. Well, apparently, it was only cold during the "winter" months, from November to March. Issata sent frequent emails, and told them all about the four seasons: Winter, Spring, Summer, and Fall. The winter was brutally cold. According to Issata, it got so cold during the winter that lakes turned into ice and people could walk on frozen water. This was hard for My and Muki to believe, but that is what they were told. Issata would elaborate in her emails...

"In April, we have a season called Spring. This is when birds fly home from their holidays down south. They start waking people up early in the morning with their songs. That's how we know the flowers are about to bloom. Summertime comes right after school is let out, from June to August. We get three entire months of summer recess oh! Summertime is very hot. In September and October, they call the season 'Fall,' when leaves on trees turn from green to orange, red and yellow. Then they fall off, leaving the trees naked."

The Broken Pump

Mymuna often daydreamed about these interesting facts and pictured herself in Issata's shoes, walking on frozen water and climbing naked trees.

In Sierra Leone, the change of seasons was known as 'Harmattan.' During Harmattan season, My and Muki covered themselves with blankets while they slept, and sometimes even covered their heads with knit hats like the ones worn by the village Chiefs. It was the time of year when some people preferred to bathe with water that had been heated on the wood fire in the outdoor kitchen. Normally, women or children were expected to boil the water. In fact, women and children were the ones found doing almost all the chores that had to do with water: collecting it, storing it, boiling it, filtering it, disinfecting it, cleaning the pots with it, washing clothes with it, and bathing children in it. Sometimes the boy children were instructed to help, but My often questioned why men did not participate in any of the water related chores, and why women and girls were expected to bear the brunt of this work. She never seemed to get a response that made much sense to her, and she was constantly asking questions about it. This seemed to annoy many adults, including her male teacher at school. But as her wise old granny Ma Musu always said, you can't change a situation with silence.

Quite frankly, My often really enjoyed walking down to the pump, because it gave her an opportunity to clear her mind. It also made her feel strong when she lifted the heavy bucket of water onto her head, and it gave her a sense of confidence and self-satisfaction to have such an important role, even if it was not appreciated by others.

"Get up Muki!" said My to her brother. "I want to be first in line when they unlock the pump." My and Muki had to queue to collect their bath water every morning from a pump down the street. They had to get there early enough to avoid the crowd; otherwise, they might be late for school. My hated missing school. She was well liked by her peers and looked up to for her smartness. She was quite confident in herself, and whatever she did seemed to be done with style. Many of the other kids envied her. My was at the top of her class, and very serious about keeping it that way.

Muki's voice was groggy as he rolled over onto his right side and curled into a ball. And as he does every morning, he lifted two fingers above his head. This was an indication to My that he needed an extra two minutes to finish his dream. Muki was a deep sleeper who often remembered his dreams and tried to figure out the meaning of them; unlike My, who was easily awoken by the call of the mosque, the cockle of the roosters, the bah of the goats, and the moo of the cows, at the first sign of dawn. Except that is, when the dream came with a message. Like the muddy river dream.

"Ok Muki, two minutes. But that's it. I have an exam today in English class. I need to get there early to meditate and clear my head, just like Ma Musu advised."

"Mmmmm... ok... I'm coming." As Muki brushed his teeth and washed his eyes out under a tree next to the outdoor kitchen, My filled Restore's food bowl with some left over rice from the night before, and his favorite treat of all... papaya! She then gathered the jerry cans that would be used to collect the water.

When they reached the pump, they were the 5th jerry can in line. But there was one problem; the line was not moving. In fact, the pump was not flowing. As more and more people came to place their jerry cans and buckets in the queue, it only became longer and longer and longer. My noticed Mister Marcus, the quiet old man who stands on the corner, people-watching and minding his own business at the same time. My greeted him: "Good Morning Pa Marcus. How are you?" Mister Marcus responded: "I'm worried Miss Mymuna. This pump has been broken since yesterday. And NOBODY knows how to fix it."

Mymuna Majik and the Broken Pump

Chapter 2: Down By The River

The river was a place of serenity. A place of gossip. A place of freedom by the virtue of nature. Time had no place by the river. People, mainly women, went there to 'brook[1]' their clothes. Usually, this was done on a Sunday, when people had come to the end of their weekend with many stories, just needing time to relax with the crackling sounds of water. The river was sacred. Some people said it was better than church or mosque because it had no expectations. People could talk, listen, or just contemplate alongside the river, and it always felt just right.

---

[1] Brook means to launder clothes in Sierra Leonean Krio language.

While people at the pump made guesses about who might have broken it, others had no time for such nonsense. They needed water. The only other pump was close to five kilometers away, a treacherous walk under the hot sun. However, there was one place in town that always had water: The River. River Shewa ran straight through the middle of Bok Town. It was one of the more popular rivers for fishing. Some people also used it for swimming, as crocodiles tended to stay away from this part of the river for some unknown reason. Of course, there were many myths floating around about why this part of the river was without crocs. Some people thought the local traditional healer, who was also My's granny, Ma Musu, had put a spell on this part of the river to keep crocodiles away. Others said this part of the river had a funny taste that the crocodiles didn't like. Hmmmm. In any case, River Shewa was more crowded than usual today, as a result of the broken pump. People washed their clothes in one section while kids bathed and brushed their teeth in another. And although the *Ministry of Health and Satisfaction* had been helping families dig their own latrines over the past few years, it was still common for people to prefer to do their toileting business in the natural stream. Some thought it was cleaner to wash their bottoms off with the cold, natural running water. Others did not like the smell of the latrines, or the flies they tended to attract. Some young kids were afraid of falling into the deep hole. Even though the kids had been learning about the benefits of using a latrine in school, they had not yet sunk in for everyone.

On this day, the situation down by the river was dire. As a result of the broken pump, people were resorting to collecting water from the bottom of the river... and DRINKING IT.

Down by the River

Chapter 3: Poo Poo Germs

Mymuna noticed something wrong with this picture.

"Do you not see what is happening here, Muki? People are poo pooing in the river all the way up there. Some of them like to climb the tree and poo poo into the river. They think the poo just disappears. But they are wrong. The germs float down the river and touch those kids who are bathing and brushing their teeth. The water then flows down to the women washing their clothes, also picking up the poo poo germs. From there, the germs float down the river to this section, where people collect water to drink. They take the water home with them, and anyone who drinks it will likely become sick with diarrhea. This can be very serious."

Mymuna had learned that this could be especially serious for children under the age of five, pregnant women, and anyone who is frequently sick.

"I don't believe you My," said Muki. "The river washes away the poo poo. I don't see any germs in this water. See?"

He held out his cupped hand where he had collected water. "It's cold, clear and SWEET!" Muki said as he slurped the water from his hand.

Mymuna was not convinced. "Don't be deceived Muki. Germs are not visible to the naked eye. I learned it in General Science class. They are so small that you cannot see them, but they are still there. If you drink the water, you will become sick."

Mymuna tried to articulate the facts in a way that would convince her brother.

But Muki continued to doubt his sister; he filled up his bucket and carried it back to the house on his head.

That night, Muki woke well before the call of the mosque, the cockle of the roosters, the bah of the goats, and the moo of the cows. His belly pained like something he'd never felt. He grabbed the lantern and raced to the latrine, nearly tripping over the bucket that was set aside for hand washing.

It was a serious case of *runbele*[2].

Muki knew his sister My was probably right, but he did not want to admit that he had drunk three cups of water earlier that day, just before My had run to tell Mama about the contaminated river water. Mama knew My was right, and replaced the river water with rainwater from the reserve tank in the back of the compound.

Unfortunately, it did not happen before Muki drank the river water. It was too late for Muki.

---

[2] Runbele means diarrhea in Sierra Leonean Krio. It comes from "runny belly."

Chapter 4: Coconut Water

The famous, well-trusted traditional healer and wisest person in Bok, who happened to be My's granny Ma Musu, came to the Majik house the next day, which happened to be a Sunday, to braid Mymuna's hair. My was very particular about her hair styles and somehow preferred Ma Musu's ability to understand just how she wanted it each week. Mymuna would think of a style that no other girl in her class would have. Sometimes it was 'double twist,' other times the Natural Fro. Today it was her favorite, zigzag plaits. She reserved her 'Rihanna' short-cut wig for special occasions. Mymuna loved being unique. It was one of her best characteristics.

Ma Musu was one of the kindest spirits in all of Bok. She loved other people's children, prayed often, and always wished well for others; something jealous people never did. She also loved to speak English and could communicate fluently in at least five of the 16 ethnic languages spoken in Sierra Leone. She was from the Shebro ethnic group, which was her Mother Tongue. In addition, she could speak Mende (the most commonly spoken traditional language in Sierra Leone), as well as Limba, Fula, and Temne. Of course, most people spoke the lingua franca Krio, a combination of multiple languages, including Bantu, English, French, and Portuguese, among others.

Not only was Ma Musu wise, tall, and beautiful, she also loved reading books and telling ancient stories passed on by the ancestors to the children after dinner, over a fire in the yard. She would cook the most delicious African food, including *plasas*, *casava leaf*, *fufu* and *okra soup*. Oh, was she a fine cook!

One of the multiple hats she wore in the community was the Academic Tutor. She would meet the children at the local library in town after school to review their homework and make sure everyone felt confident in their ability to do well on tests. Education was an especially important topic for Ma Musu, as she herself was denied the right to education, but learned anyway. Just like Dr. Tererai Trent, the social activist from Zimbabwe, who was denied education because she was a girl, and then, buried her dreams to get an education in a can, and her wishes came true! She then wrote about it in the award-winning book "The Girl Who Buried Her Dreams in a Can," and gave back to her community by raising funds for quality schools, nutritious canteens, and academic scholarships for girls.

Along with a bag full of fresh fruit such as oranges, bananas, or mangoes, Ma Musu often came to the library with a baby or two on her back, as she was also the "go-to" person for childcare. And the most special thing about Ma Musu was a secret that only Mymuna was aware of: her ability to communicate with Barack the Crock, the River Guardian... Just. Like. Mymuna.

After Mymuna explained to Ma Musu about Muki's diarrhea, the Traditional Healer/Hair Stylist/Tutor/Caregiver said that she had already heard about the outbreak. She had just been to three other houses with cases of *runbele*.

Ma Musu made haste in her decision to call an emergency meeting with the Community Health Club. She went knocking on the door of the town Chief and Mami Queen and told them about the predicament. They immediately notified the 'Town Crier' who used her megaphone and bicycle, donated by Haqq Enterprise - a local business headquartered in the capital city of Freetown - to ride around and call for people to attend the meeting.

One hour later, while sitting in a circle under the central Palava Hut[3], the Chief asked one of the Muslims to lead a prayer. The community members held out their hands and collectively recited the prayer in Arabic. When they finished, he asked a Christian to lead a prayer. There was one Jewish family in the community who had moved to Sierra Leone from Ethiopia. The mother of that family then read a prayer in Hebrew. The meeting was now officially open, and the Chief began speaking:

"As you know, we have a serious outbreak on our hands. Too many people have *runbele*. Ma Musu, please take the floor."

Ma Musu spoke with authority and compassion, "If you or your *pikenden*[4] get *runbele*, the best thing you can do is make them drink coconut water. This will make sure they do not get too dehydrated, which can be very dangerous and even deadly. We need to move fast and harvest as many coconuts as possible. We will delegate a few of the older kids to climb the trees. We will then need wheel barrels to carry the coconuts to distinct locations where people can easily access them."

Koro Thoro, My's uncle and community health club officer, raised his hand to speak: "Thank you Ma Musu. You are right. We will need to mobilize and set up 'coconut corners' until this outbreak is under control. Two community health club officers will work in each of the corners. We will rotate shifts of four hours each. Community members can chip in by providing them with fruit such as bananas and oranges. Community health club officers will also need to up the ante in educating people about the root causes of *runbele*."

---

[3] A palava hut is a traditionally built community gathering space where important meetings are held and decisions made for the benefit of the entire community.
[4] Piken = child; pikenden = children in Krio.

Fatu, another community health club officer, added: "We'll need to make sure everyone knows that they should get to the nearest clinic if they have *runbele* more than three times a day, or if they have *runbele* with fever."

Mymuna was standing by: "Excuse me, I would like to say something please."

Ma Musu turned around. "Yes, My, what is it?"

"Well, I think you should also warn people not to drink water from the river. I figured out why people are getting *runbele*. You see, that pump down the street has not worked in three days. People have started drinking the river water instead of the safe water from the pump. That river water is used by many people for defecating. That is why people are getting sick."

Koro Thoro replied, "Well my young niece, you are a smart girl, I have taught you well. And she is right everyone. That river should not be used for drinking. People need to know that if they cannot get water from the pump, they should use the rainwater they have been saving all year."

Mister Marcus intervened, "I don't collect rainwater, I didn't think it was safe."

Koro Thoro replied, "Rainwater is a gift. It is natural and safe. If you make sure to collect it in a clean container, it is safe. If you want to be extra sure, you can filter or boil it. Boiling water for at least two minutes can help kill any germs."

"Is there anyone willing to spare their coconuts for the sake of this outbreak?"

That afternoon, there was an organized chaos in Bok town. People were climbing trees, harvesting drinking coconuts, putting them in wheel barrels and pushing them to the delegated spots to be used as 'coconut corners.' Other community members carried baskets of oranges and bananas on their heads to bring to the corners. Community health club officers tended the corners, educating community members about diarrhea and the importance of staying hydrated. They also warned people not to drink river water and advised they only drink water from a protected pump or the sky.

Then, the organized chaos began to get out of hand. While harvesting the coconuts, My and one of her best friends, Sitotah, accidentally dropped a coconut on the foot of an innocent by-stander.

"Eh Bo!" shouted the bystander, jumping up and down as he held his foot in agony.

"Sorry," My said, climbing down from the tree. "I was just collecting these for my brother who is sick with *runbele*. I am on my way home to make sure he gets rehydrated with the coconut water."

Muki had already missed two days of school after visiting the clinic and was told to drink coconut water, safe water with oral rehydration salt, or sugar salt solution: 1 liter of water + 8 teaspoons of sugar + half teaspoon of salt.

"Hi Muki," My said as she walked into the family house. "How de body?" (How are you?).

"Tell God Tenki[5]. I'm a bit better," Muki replied.

"Well, I got these coconuts for you," said My, holding two coconuts, one in each hand.

"Thank you," said Muki.

Mister Majik took the cutlass and hacked off the top of the coconut for Muki to drink.

After drinking the second coconut, Muki felt much better. "I'll return to school tomorrow!!" he said with excitement.

---

[5] A common Krio response to a greeting meaning, "Give thanks to God."

Later that day, as Mymuna carried a load of clothes on her head after washing them down at the river hole, she caught a glimpse of her confidant, Barack the Crock, out of the corner of her eye. And just as Barack always does, he winked one eye at Mymuna before submersing.

That was a sign that, once again, Mymuna Majik was right.

Chapter 5: Muddy Waters

The next day, as people went down to the river to collect their water for drinking, cooking and bathing, they arrived with a shock to their eyes.

The river was mud. Not only mud, but a bright, florescent purple mud – thick and glaring to the eye. The water was gone. Replaced with something so strange and scary, people ran at first sight of the spectacular phenomenon.

Mymuna went to her special spot along the river near the waterfall to see if Barack the Crock was there. She had a feeling he might have something to do with the muddy river.

Barack was there, waiting to give Mymuna her message.

"Barack! What is happening to the river? People are desperate for water but it has turned into this bright purple mud."

Barack smirked at Mymuna before responding. "And what did you predict My? You were telling Muki about it yesterday."

My responded, "That people would get sick from drinking the river water, because they were using it for pooping, bathing, and washing clothes upstream."

That's right. I needed to protect this river, and to protect the people who got sick from it – like your brother Mukpasi did. This was the only way to prevent them from drinking it.

My thought for a minute and then said, "There are multiple solutions to this problem that can work together. We find a way to fix the pump. And we start using safe water sources more, like catching the rainwater as a back-up, in case the pump breaks again. And, we must teach people how to fix the pump so that if it does break, we are not forced to go to the river."

"You have the answers right there inside of you, as always 'Smart One.' And who do you know that can help?"

My smiled a huge grin with her bright sparkling teeth. "My Uncle, Koro Thoro," replied My.

"Once I feel the respect for the river again, I will restore it to the precious water source that everyone cherishes. Something of that level of beauty deserves to be honored for its worth," Barack the Crock contended.

Chapter 6: Fix the Pump

Mymuna presented her idea to her uncle, making a clear statement about the need to fix the pump and rally the community to prevent these problems from occurring in the future. This, she suggested, required free community training in pump maintenance and long term sustainability, to anyone interested, especially women and girls.

As a leader of the Community Health Club, Koro Thoro was proud to help out and said, "We have decent savings in our Osusu (Savings and Loan) Club from all of the contributions from members. This is exactly the type of thing we should be spending our money on. Good thinking Mymuna!"

The community health club officers developed a plan to locate and buy the parts required to fix the pump.

Mymuna and Mukpasi worked with Uncle Thoro to recruit the best technicians to identify the problem and fix the pump. That meant, they would have to do some assessing. My advised they all use a gender-equitable lens while interviewing candidates for the job. This was important in anything and everything one did, as mandated by the Sierra Leonean Government.

"We need to be sure not to only select boys and men, just because that is the way we've seen it done in the past. We know there are plenty women and girls who are more than capable of engineering, even though it is not the typical stereotype. Time for that story to end!" urged My.

Muki said he agreed, and told them about a presentation he viewed in social studies on sexism, misogyny, and patriarchy.

A group of local water, sanitation and hygiene (WASH) technicians who had attended the Bok Technical Training Institute and learned how to install and maintain pumps, offered to conduct a training of community members on how to fix the pump should it ever break again.

A pair of female identical twins named Wata and Yata, as well as two young males named Habib and Wajid, all graduates at the top of their class at the technical college, volunteered to conduct the training, with food and a small stipend provided by the community health club officers.

My attended the training.

To open the three-day, hands-on workshop, Wata asked the group, "Does anyone know why we are here today?"

My quickly jumped in with a response in a matter-of-fact tone, "To learn how to fix the pump!"

"Ok My, you are right," Wata said.

"Like always," Yata murmured under her breath.

"Why do WE need to learn how to fix it?" said Small, one of the little kids who lived near the pump.

"Well, remember the recent outbreak caused as a result of the broken pump?" said Habib.

Small looked down at his feet and shrugged his shoulders, "So what?"

"Well, what do you think we should do little man? Wait around until the Good Witch of the North comes to fix it?"

Small gasped, "Whooooooooo???!!!"

"Never mind," said Habib. "... Let us get started! Too many people got sick when our pump broke recently. We don't want it to happen again."

After opening the pump with the wrench, Habib jumped back.

A pangolin crawled out of the pipe! It must have gotten stuck and was blocking the water from coming out. By removing the part it was stuck in, Habib freed the scared pangolin.

One of the old men in the village ran to get a machete to kill the pangolin and have it for dinner.

"We must kill it and grill it, make haste!" said the old man.

Mymuna did not think it was necessary to kill animals just for the sake of eating them, if there was other food available, which was the current case in Bok. The community had put together a food drying and jarring system to preserve food year round. They always had an abundance of beans, millet, ground nut paste, cassava bread and fruit juices like pineapple, mango, and papaya. It made My's mouth water just thinking about it.

She then reached down to gently pick up the pangolin, sending it into the forest nearby, before the old man could get his hands on it.

"Ayeeeeeeek!" squeaked the elder. "My Gooooooodness!"

Habib showed My how to close the pump back up using the tools in the tool kit. My was so happy to have this new skill and decided she wanted to be an engineer when she grew up. That was her new dream. And she would be sharing it with Barack the Crock, who could make dreams come true... only if you had faith of course. Just like Dr. Tererai Trent from Zimbabwe did, showing us that anything is possible.

Mymuna's new dream was to install many more pumps throughout the town, and to teach people how to collect rainwater, Mother Earth's most precious gift.

Chapter 7: Prevention

Mymuna went to her secret spot along the crackling river, behind a large rock next to a small waterfall, to seek advice from Barack the Crock. As she sat down in her happy place, pondering the diarrhea dilemma, she spoke aloud:

"Why does diarrhea continue to be such a big problem in this community? Even when the pump works, people still get sick. If only there was some other way we could stop people from getting diarrhea, the people in this community would be much healthier and happier."

Just then, she heard the bubbling under the water, and saw a light spray as Barack the Crock's head immerged from the surface of the crisp, clear, sun-sparkled water.

"Good thinking My. Once again, your brightness comes through."

"Oh, hi Barack! I'm so glad to see you."

"I am proud to see you thinking about prevention, not just coconuts, laughed Barack."

"What do you mean?"

"Well, you hit on something the other day when you were at the town meeting. You told the community members that you discovered why people were getting sick."

"Yes, well, they were drinking contaminated river water. Like you said."

"No, you discovered it. I only agreed with you."

"Oh?"

"And, you have the very answer to your question right there inside of you. All you have to do is…"

Mymuna finished his sentence… "Just stay calm."

"Absolutely 100% Correct!" exclaimed Barack.

Mymuna sat with her feet in the water and closed her eyes, as he led her breathing in for three seconds… 1… 2… 3…; holding for four seconds… 1…2…3…4; and out for five seconds… 1…2…3…4…5. Repeat.

Mymuna focused on her breath while observing her senses. She felt the cool tickle of the small ripples in the water around her ankles, little nibbles from the tiny fish on her toes, and the soothing rhythm of the birds chirping, like a song written just for her.

Then, she immediately recalled something she had learned in Health Education class last semester. It was one of her favorite classes, and she got a 75%, which was distinction, and put her in the top of the class. It was the grade that put her in the lead, ahead of Ahmed Ali Amen, nicknamed "Triple A."

Normally, My was on a battle ground with Triple A for 'Number One Student.' Last year, he beat her by one percentage point. The previous year, she won by two percentage points. The year before, they called it a tie and gave them each a scholarship, which is the typical award for the Number One Student at the end of each school year. 'The Year of the Tie' was an unprecedented decision; even making top news on Salone Radio, the national radio station.

It was the last assignment of the school year that instructed students to come up with key messages to prevent people from getting diarrhea. My's uncle, Koro Thoro, a community health club officer, had talked to her in depth about the F diagram: feces (poo poo), fingers, flies, fields, fluids (rivers), and food. She knew the diagram by heart. It demonstrated all of the possible points of fecal contamination that can lead to people getting sick with diarrhea. She had presented and explained the diagram to her class, showing how people can create barriers to germ transmission by practicing hygienic behaviors such as handwashing after using the latrine and before touching food, covering food to prevent flies, and avoiding drinking water from the river and other unprotected sources. She then turned the diagram into a life sized game with pictures that the Community Health Club used in their health education sessions. That was what got her the top grade.

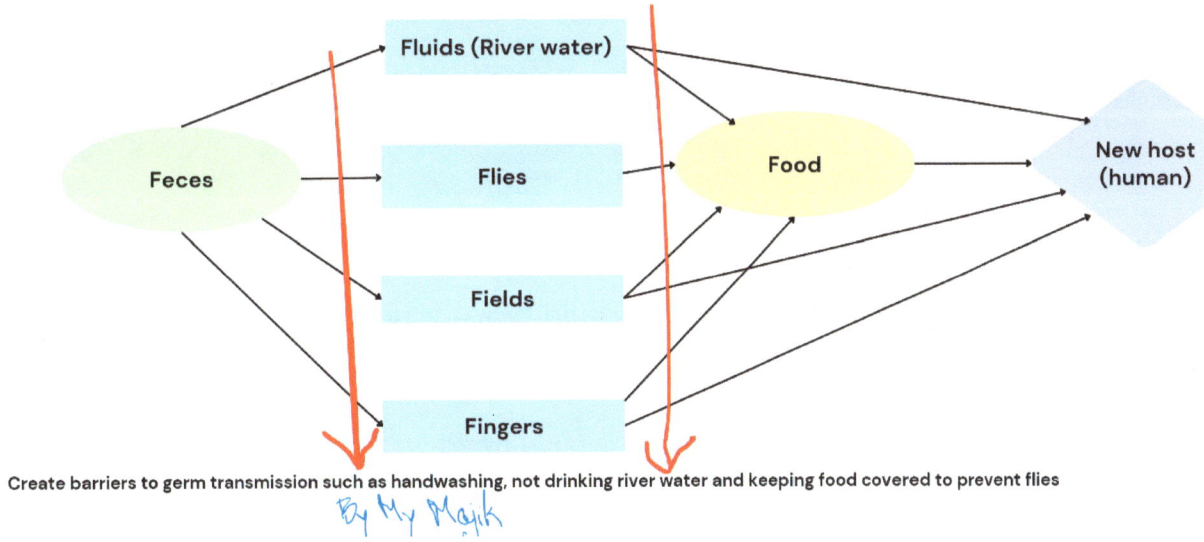

Create barriers to germ transmission such as handwashing, not drinking river water and keeping food covered to prevent flies

By My Majik

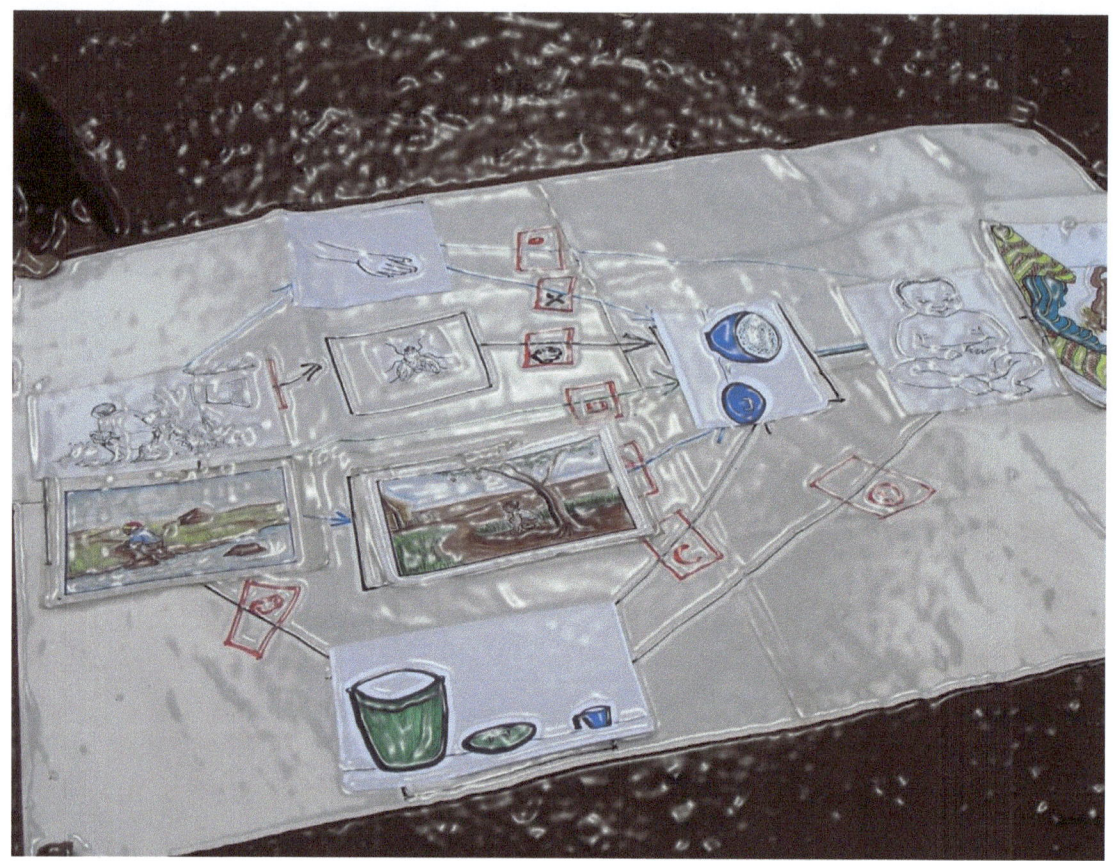

Mymuna thought back to the diagram and figured this would be an ideal time to use it. She reflected on the barriers that could prevent people from getting diarrhea. One way was to make sure people wash their hands after they use the latrine. But there was a problem. Most latrines did not have hand washing facilities next to them. People would have to walk back to their homes and use their drinking water containers for washing their hands after using the latrine. This could contaminate the drinking water. More likely, they would just forget to wash their hands altogether. Then the next time they went to eat, they would get germs on their food. Or, they would spread the germs to anything they touched. Simply by putting their hands near their mouths after using the latrine could make them ill. Now how on earth could this problem be solved?

My opened her eyes and said to Barack:

"We need to round up the community to get serious about diarrhea. We need to start getting people excited about handwashing, protecting water, and keeping the environment clean!"

"Mmmhmmm"... said Barack.

"But you know, those community health workers have been telling people to wash their hands for years, even when your parents were your age."

"Really?" said Mymuna.

"Then why hasn't the situation changed?"

All of a sudden, out of nowhere, or perhaps somewhere unknown (what's the difference?), a revelation sprang upon her!

This tended to happen when she sat with Barack. She would see a spark just above her brow bone, and would look up to see a sign. It could be a sign of any kind. Even a Stop Sign.

This time, it was a bird. A Sankofa bird. Its head was looking back with an egg in its beak, and its feet were facing forward.

Everyone knew that the Sankofa bird was an old African adage, symbolizing the importance of grieving, retrieving, and honoring the past, "For therein lies the future," someone famous once said. The Sankofa bird warns that, if one forgets the lessons of the past, they are destined to repeat them.

Mymuna looked at Barack and said, "We need to look at what's REALLY the problem. For YEARS, people have been learning about the importance of handwashing. We learn it in school and in the clinics."

"The PROBLEM is... most latrines in this community do not have handwashing facilities," she continued.

She decided that was it! They needed to mobilize materials and build hand washing facilities next to each and every latrine.

Barack agreed and gave her his famous wink before submerging again.

Mymuna talked to Uncle Koro about this and he organized a meeting with the Community Health Club to discuss the issue. At first, most of the club members said it was the government's responsibility and they would not pay even one Leone for a hand washing facility. Fatu spoke up and said, "If we keep sitting around waiting for the government to fix all of our problems, we will continue to see our people get sick and die."

Koro Thoro supported her. "We know this is preventable, and the solution is not difficult. All we need is to mobilize some buckets, ash from the stoves to be used as soap, cups for rinsing and a sturdy table to place the buckets."

The Chief cut in... "And each family will designate two people to be responsible for filling the buckets at the end of each day using rain or pump water." Mami Queen intervened... "And this must not only be the women and children. Men need to play a part here as well." The Chief nodded, hesitantly.

The community health club officers agreed that this would not be that hard. But they also knew it would take some work.

Ma Musu summarized it: "Think of it this way, we can sit around and do nothing, and continue to get sick, OR... we make sure we only drink water from safe sources - like the protected pump or the heavenly sky. And, we make sure everyone washes their hands with soap or ash at all of the important times. This will improve our lives.

This is a hard working community. We could be the healthiest, most satisfied community in all of Sierra Leone if we wanted. Isn't it so?"

"Ma Musu, this is a very timely message. Next week is World Water Week!" proclaimed Wata.

"The Community Health Club is holding more workshops on how to maintain your pump. This will include what to do any time the pump breaks or is not working properly."

Yata continued... "Every pump will have a monitor assigned, who will be responsible for fixing the pump shall it break. Each neighborhood will need to establish a water committee, to ensure the pump is always working and report it if it stops."

The community health officers also organized a team to cut local bamboo growing plentifully in the nearby forest. The bamboo was used to build solid fences around the community pumps to keep the animals out. Native flowers and vines were planted alongside the bamboo to beautify the pumps and keep them sacred.

The following Sunday, the Community Health Club met in the palava hut under the Bok Central Baobab Tree, Africa's Tree of Life. They began with a check-in, where they each took turns sharing out three things they felt grateful for. Every single person said they were grateful for one thing in particular, in common: Water. They ended the meeting with a brand new set of bylaws intended to preserve and protect the pump, the river, the environment, the animals, and the people ever-so-blessed to live amongst them.

Over the next few months, the town of Bok would see a reduction in diarrheal disease and improvements in overall health and satisfaction... and it wasn't magic (but something like that).

What bylaws would you put in place to protect the pump, the river, the environment, the animals and the people?

_____

_____

_____

_____

KEY LESSONS FROM THIS STORY:

1. Always use a safe source for drinking water such as a protected pump.

2. If the pump breaks, choose a safe alternative such as rainwater.

3. If there is no safe alternative and you must use water from the river or stream, make sure to filter it or boil it for at least two minutes before drinking.

4. Drinking water from young coconuts can help cure diarrhea.

5. It is important to go to the clinic right away if fever presents, or if someone has had three or more loose stools in 24 hours.

6. Always wash your hands after toileting and before eating or preparing food.

What else did you learn?

_____

_____

_____

Did you know?...

- ❖ Diarrheal disease is the third leading cause of death in children under five years old worldwide. It is both preventable and treatable.
- ❖ The simple act of washing hands with soap or ash at critical moments – such as after poo pooing or pee peeing, or before touching food – is an easy and affordable intervention that can reduce the incidence of diarrhea.

References:

WHO: https://www.who.int/news-room/fact-sheets/detail/diarrhoeal-disease

UNICEF: https://data.unicef.org/topic/child-health/diarrhoeal-disease/

Mymuna Majik and the Broken Pump

Photo credits:

Palava hut, p.19: Moses Bockarie

Wheelbarrow with coconuts, p.23: Moses Bockarie

Person drinking coconut, side view, p.24: Ishamil Barrie

Person drinking coconut with pink shirt, p. 26: Sulaiman Kamara

All other photos: KAZ

www.ingramcontent.com/pod-product-compliance
Lightning Source LLC
Chambersburg PA
CBHW060821090426
42738CB00002B/62